ROMAN ROADS
OF
HAMPSHIRE

Alex Vincent

MP Middleton Press

Published October 2005

ISBN 1 904474 67 5

© Middleton Press, 2005

Design Emily Pede

Published by
    Middleton Press
    Easebourne Lane
    Midhurst, West Sussex
    GU29 9AZ
Tel: 01730 813169
Fax: 01730 812601
Email: info@middletonpress.co.uk
www.middletonpress.co.uk

Printed & bound by Biddles Ltd, Kings Lynn

CONTENTS

ACKNOWLEDGEMENTS

I wish to thank the Hampshire Field Club and Archaeological Society and the Havant Museum for their help in preparing this book. Much appreciation also goes to Mr D. and Dr S. Salter and C. Webb for help in proof reading.

The general arrangement of Roman roads in Hampshire, with Margary's numbers.

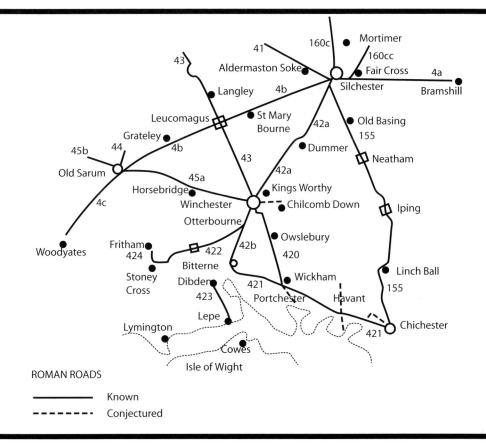

1. INTRODUCTION

There were some 10,000 miles of Roman roads in Britain of which about 7500 miles are known, with another 2500 or so yet to be proved and possibly many more still to be discovered. Most construction of Roman roads was done during the first century AD. Some of these roads were military, some for commercial use and others were purely local.

Roman roads were mainly built straight, but not from start to finish as there were changes in direction en-route particularly where they descended hills on terraceways. Purely local Roman roads were not necessarily straight and where the terrain was very hilly with steep sided valleys, a straight road would not be possible and would have to have curves in many places. Many Roman roads joined and crossed each other in cities, but some junctions were in the countryside.

Width and surfaces of roads varied a great deal from one region to another. Most main Roman roads were some 20-23 feet wide, but could have been more if traffic increased. Most were on a nine foot agger or embankment, with ditches on either side. Materials used on roads depended on what was available in the area. Chalk and flint for example was used in southern England and Limestone in the north and west. Most Roman roads were paved.

There were no paved roads in Britain, apart from a few timbered causeways, before the Roman period; they were just tracks. Not all Roman roads were paved because if the soil was well drained then paving would not have been necessary and this also applies to purely local roads as well. The spoil from cuttings would have been used for embankments.

Roman roads were built to give access to the Roman settlements across Britain and to connect towns and cities. Some were provided with posting stations or mansios, which were placed at intervals of between 12 and 15 miles, as this represented a day's travelling. Posting stations consisted of an embanked area some 2½ to 4 acres in a rectangle. They comprised an inn, stables and a few houses.

Roman roads crossed rivers, streams and estuaries by means of either a bridge, ford or ferry. The Romans preferred to ford and so most were forded and those on foot had wet feet, whilst some waded up to their waist. Some fords were paved such as at Iden Green in Kent. An estuary was crossed by a ferry, as were the Rivers Adur and Arun in Sussex. Other waterways were crossed by a bridge where wooden piles were driven into a river bed, such as at Alfoldean on Stane Street in Sussex.

A great number of Roman roads are still visible today either as an agger (embankment), hollow way (cutting), a terraceway on a hill or simply hedgerows. Treelines, footpaths and modern roads also mark their course. Others are not visible above ground due to erosion, extensive ploughing or developments such as housing. Those not visible on the ground may sometimes be seen from the air and aerial photography has revealed many sites.

Mr I.D.Margary (1896-1976) specialised in the study of Roman roads. He discovered the line of a Roman road, between Chuck Hatch near Hartfield and Camp Hill near Duddleswell, on aerial photographs which he had taken of the Ashdown Forest in 1929. This was the London to Lewes Roman road and after this, Margary visited all known sites throughout the country. He wrote a number of books and many articles recording his findings. He gave all Roman roads reference numbers from Watling Street (No. 1), Ermine Street (No. 2), The Great Road (No. 3) and so on.

The London to Lewes Road is Margary's No. 14 and its associated branches such as the Sussex Greensand Way (Barcome Mills to Hardham) is No. 140, Pevensey to Glynde is No. 142 etc. Stane Street (London to Chichester) is Margary's No. 15 and its associated branches such as the London to Brighton Roman road is No. 150, the Chichester to Silchester is No. 155. In other words Roman road No. 14 is a branch of No. 4 and No. 142 is a branch of No. 14.

Where the Roman road was long, it is divided by letters in the lower case such as Watling Street, (Dover to Wroxeter), where the section from Dover to Canterbury is Margary's No. 1a, Canterbury to Rochester No. 1b, Rochester to London 1c etc. If there are two or more parallel Roman roads divided by letters, then one is double lettered, for example Dorchester to Silchester is Margary's No. 160c and Dorchester to Fair Cross east of Silchester is No. 160cc. These numbers are used throughout this book.

There are many names that can suggest a Roman route, such as Street, Streat, Streatham, Stratton, Stratford, Coldharbour and Wickham. Also Ridgeway, Causeway, Green Street, Folly Hill and Ford names are worth looking into. Names like Stan, Stane, Stanstead, Strett and Stone may have derived from the stony nature of a Roman road. Places in Britain with these names may well occur near or on the line of a possible Roman road.

This book gives details of all the Roman roads in Hampshire, starting with its title, Margary number, length in miles, description of the route, maps and photographs (taken by the author). There are 16 of them and at the end of the book there is a section on other Roman roads which may exist, as well as other tracks which are dotted all over the county.

The Ordnance Survey maps herein are at the scale of 1ins to 1 mile and north is at the top, except where rotation of the place names indicates otherwise. They were all published in the late 1940s, when there was less building development to hinder the study of Roman roads. Many of their alignments are marked thereon, as understood at that time. The existence of a footpath on these maps does not necessarily indicate a right of way and thus current maps and signposts must be used to determine this fact. Many of the locations described are on private property and consent must be obtained before entering onto such land. The recent "Right to Roam" legislation has many limitations and is not what its popular title suggests. The numbers in black circles on the maps indicate the locations of the relevant photographs.

The A272 west of Winchester has recently been renumbered B3049 and part of the B3420 has become the A272. The A34 northwest of Winchester is now the B3420. Thus the maps and text may differ in this area. It also applies elsewhere to some extent.

2. LONDON TO SILCHESTER (The Devil's Highway)
(4a) 44 miles

This Roman road was an important highway, linking London with the southwest of England. It left London at Newgate and went in a southwesterly direction through Hammersmith, Brentford (where it passed the northern end of the big bend in the River Thames), Hounslow and Staines.

At Staines, the Roman road crossed the Thames on more than one bridge as the name of Staines means Pontes, "The Bridges". The position of these bridges and Roman road here is not known, but could have been at a point just south of where the A30 crosses the river. West of the crossing the Roman road (known as The Devil's Highway from here to Silchester), went through Engelfield Green, Virginia Water and Sunningdale.

At Sunningdale, the Roman road exists as an agger along a treeline, then the route ran along the Surrey/Berkshire border for about two miles, entering the latter north of Bagshot. From here the road ran along a track and footpath in a wooded area to Crowthorne, where it is lost due to development, and went through Finchampstead and then crossed the rivers Blackwater and Whitewater on a ford at Bramshill. A ford exists at this point today and the Roman road entered Hampshire just east of it.

West of the ford, the Roman road ran along the Berkshire/Hampshire border to the south of Riseley, where a footpath marks its course, Stanford End and Fair Cross, where the Dorchester to Fair Cross Roman road (Margary's No. 160cc) joined it. From here the route is marked by a footpath north of Wigmore Farm, for about two miles, to Butlers Lands, then along Park Lane, where it entered wholly into Hampshire. It then ran along another footpath for a while and entered the Roman town of Calleva Atrebatum (Silchester) at the east gate.

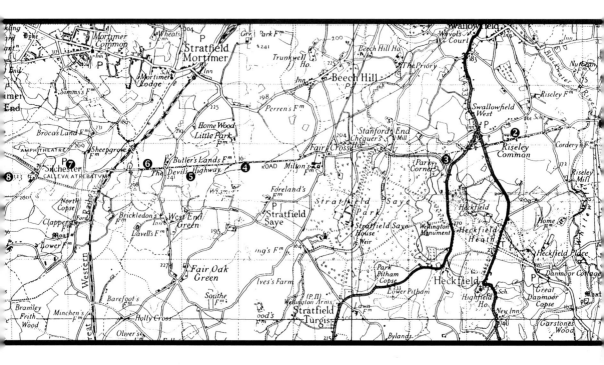

2.1 **Site of ford on the London to Silchester Roman road at the existing ford at Bramshill.**

2.2 **The Roman road known as "The Devil's Highway" along a line east of Riseley.**

2.3   The site of the road across a field west of Riseley.

2.4   The Roman road as a footpath north of Wigmore Farm.

2.5   *The road along a footpath at Butlers Lands.*

2.6   *The road along a lane at Butlers Lands.*

2.7   *The route marked by a footpath across a field east of Silchester.*

2.8   Site of the road across a field at Silchester.

2.9   The London to Silchester Roman road through the Roman town of Calleva Atrebatum at Silchester.

3. SILCHESTER TO OLD SARUM

(Portway)
(4b) 36¼ miles

The Roman road from London continued from Silchester, leaving the Roman town at the southwest gate and went in a southwesterly direction through the Pamber Forest (where trees mark its course), crossed the A340 south of Tadley and it is then marked by a footpath at Skate's Farm. West of the farm the route went across fields and through woodland near Browninghill

Green, Stony Heath, Foscot Farm and then crossed the A339 southeast of Kingsclere. After this the Roman road went over downland north of Hannington and then along a minor road for about 1½ miles to the north of Polhampton Lodge.

From here, the route ran along a Lane at Robley Belt for about ¾ mile and then it is marked by a footpath for about three miles at Caesar's Belt, running parallel with woodland. The Roman road then crossed the A34 at Clap Gate, went through Bradley Wood, where it is visible as an agger for about ½ mile, continuing along hedgerows across fields to St. Mary Bourne where it crossed the B3048. West of St Mary Bourne the Roman road ascended a hill where a footpath marks its

3.1 *The Roman road "Portway" ran across a field in Silchester.*

3.2 *The Portway marked by a trackway through the Pamber Forest.*

3.3   The line of the Roman road "Portway" across a valley near Hannington.

course, followed by lanes from Middle
Wyke Farm to Finkley and across a field
to East Anton near Andover.

At East Anton, the route crossed the
Winchester to Wanborough Roman road
(Margary's No. 43) at the small Roman
town of Leucomagus where there are
humps and bumps in a field marking its
site. In Andover, the Roman road is lost
due to development and a minor road
marks it west of the town; it went across
a field, through Monxton village, along
a lane south of Amport and then through
woodland, where there is an agger. West
of this, the route went across fields north
of Grateley and along a footpath where
it entered Wiltshire at Hampshire Gap,
some two miles to the west. The Roman
road continued along a footpath to
Porton, then along a minor road through
Winterbourne and entered the east gate
of the Roman town of Sorviodunum at
Old Sarum, north of Salisbury.

*3.4   Portway along a footpath at
the eastern end of Caesar's Belt*

3.5   Portway along a treeline at Caesars Belt.

3.6   Hollow way of the Portway in a field near Egbury.

3.7   *Portway marked by a footpath west of St. Mary Bourne.*

3.8   *Agger of Portway north of Finkley Manor.*

3.9   *Portway along a treeline at the site of the small Roman town of Leucomagus at East Anton, Andover.*

3.10   *The route of Portway along a lane through the village of Monxton.*

3.11   Portway visible as an agger in woodland near Amport.

3.12   Portway along a minor road and footpath at Grateley.

4. OLD SARUM TO BADBURY RINGS
(4c) 21¾ miles

This section of the southwest route from London left Old Sarum at the south gate and went in a southwesterly direction through Salisbury, Netherhampton, across a golf course on a footpath, and then a lane marks its course to Stratford Tony. From here, the route crossed the River Ebble, from whence it is marked by a farm lane and is visible as a terrace-way on the east side of a deep combe.

The Roman road continued over downland and then a footpath marks its course at Knighton Wood, where it entered Hampshire, running close to the Wiltshire border for 1½ miles along a footpath on the eastern side of Vernditch Chase on an agger. At the southern end of the copse, the Roman road went across fields on a remarkable agger for about 500 yards and then entered Dorset north of Woodyates.

At this point, the route ran across a field west of the A354 to Woodyates for about 1½ miles, where the main road marks it . South of this the Roman road is visible as an outstanding agger known as "The Ackling Dyke", over the Dorset Downs, then it is marked by lanes and footpaths to Badbury Rings where the Badbury Rings to Kingston Deverell Roman road (Margary's No. 46) joined it.

4.1   *The Old Sarum to Badbury Rings Roman road along a treelined agger near Knighton Wood.*

4.2   *Agger of the Roman road at the southern end of Vernditch Chase.*

4.3   *The remarkable agger of the Old Sarum to Badbury Rings Roman road across a field north of Woodyates.*

5. SILCHESTER TO SPEEN
(41a) 12 miles

This Roman road left the Roman town of Calleva Atrebatum (Silchester) at the west gate and went in a northwesterly direction where it is marked as a footpath for a short while. It continued over a field, crossed a minor road and went through Frith Woods north of Silchester Common, where it is visible as an agger. The route then progressed along Soke Road at Aldermaston Soke where it entered Berkshire.

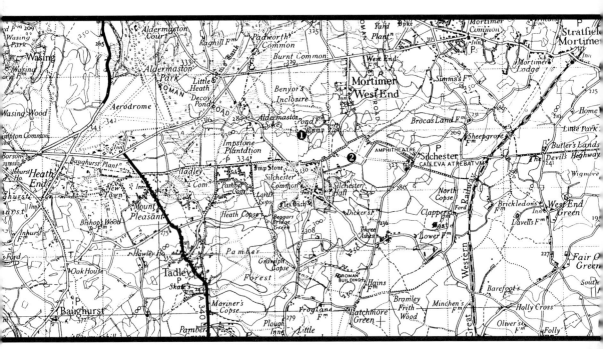

From here, the route traversed a field, crossed the Grim's Bank at Little Heath, through Aldermaston Park and Wasing Park where it is visible as an agger. After the park the Roman road went along a minor road, then crossed the Rivers Enbourne near Shalford Farm and Kennet south of Midgham, where it changed direction to the west, through Thatcham to Speen near Newbury. The section of this Roman road west of Speen to Gloucester via Cirencester is known as Ermin Street.

5.1 *Silchester to Speen Roman road along a treelined footpath at the Roman town of Calleva Atrebatum near Silchester.*

5.2 *The Roman road across a field west of Silchester.*

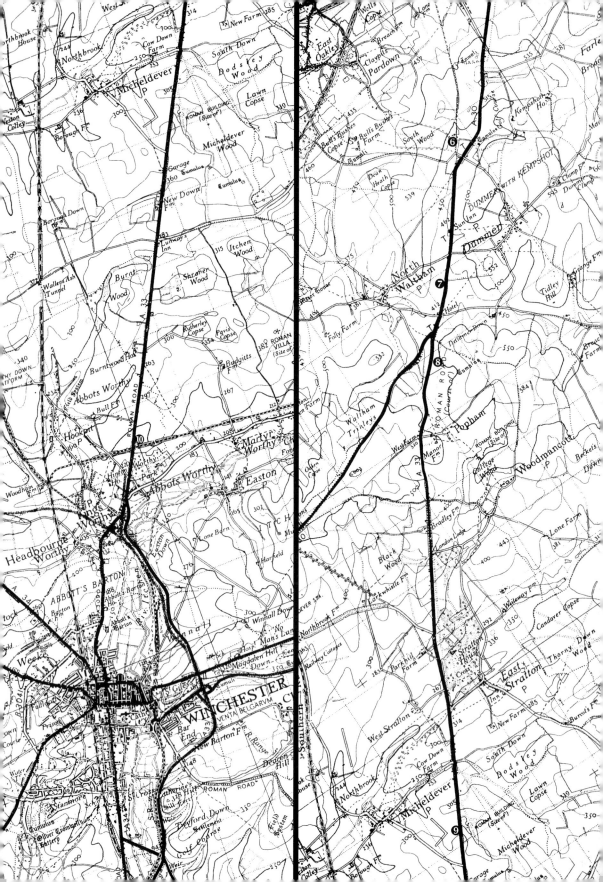

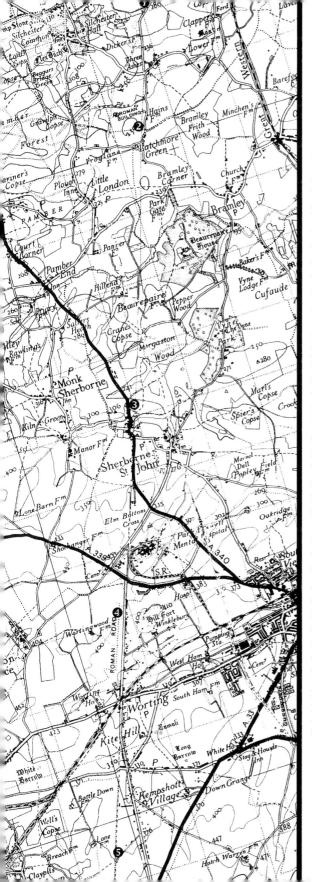

6. SILCHESTER TO WINCHESTER
(42a) 22½ miles

This Roman road was an important route to Winchester which left Silchester at the south gate and followed an almost direct course with one change of direction north of Dummer. Just south of Silchester, the route is marked by a road for ¾ mile, then went across fields west of the road via Three Ashes, Hains Farm where the Chichester to Silchester Roman road (Margary's No. 155) joined it, and Latchmore Green. From here the route went across fields and woodland to Sherborne St. John where the A340 runs along its course for ½ mile.

South of Sherborne St. John the Roman road is marked by a footpath, where there is a well preserved agger for about a mile before crossing the A339. The route is then marked by a minor road aptly named "Roman Road" to Worting, where it passed under the main line railway from Southampton to London, from here a footpath marks its course west of a built up area on the outskirts of Basingstoke, for about two miles to the southwest of Kempshott. The route then crossed a field on a treelined agger, through a strip of woodland, where it changed direction more to the southwest near South Wood Farm, north of Dummer.

South of the farm, the Roman road ran along the A30 east of North Waltham for about a mile, then over a field, along a hedge line, from where the route is lost due to the M3 junction with the A303. South of this at West Farm it is visible as an agger across a field, and then the A33 marks its course to Kings Worthy via Stratton and Micheldever, which is very much raised in places, often by three or four feet. South of Kings Worthy the Roman road ran straight to Winchester, across a field on a treeline via Abbot's Barton on the western side of the River Itchen and entered the Roman town of Venta Belgarum at the north gate where a plaque marks its site.

6.1   *The Silchester to Winchester Roman road as it left the south gate of Calleva Atrebatum at Silchester.*

6.2   *Site of the Roman road across a field at Latchmore Green.*

6.3 *Earthwork of the Roman road north of Sherborne St. John.*

6.4 *The route along the aptly named street "Roman Road" on the western outskirts of Basingstoke.*

6.5 *The Roman road marked by hedgerows near Hatch Warren. The route can be seen going into the distance.*

6.6 *The Roman road in woodland north of South Wood Farm.*

6.7 **The route marked by a hedgeline at North Waltham.**

6.8   The   Roman road along a hedgerow at West Farm, Popham.

6.9   The   route along the A33 south of Micheldever.

6.10   *The raised bank of the Roman road on the A33 north of Kings Worthy.*

6.11   *Site of north gate Winchester, where the Silchester to Winchester Roman road entered the Roman town of Venta Belgarum. A plaque marks the site.*

7. WINCHESTER TO BITTERNE
(42b) 9 miles

The road from Silchester continued southwards from Winchester along the western side of the Itchen valley. It left Winchester at the south gate and ran straight along the B3335 via St Cross where the main line railway tunnels through it. The Roman road then ran to the west of a minor road at Compton where it is visible as an agger, along the road through the village. South of Compton the M3 crosses the route at Shawford.

South of Shawford, the Roman road ran along a minor road at South Down to Otterbourne where the Otterbourne to Stoney Cross Roman road (Margary's No. 422) joined it. The route then went across a field where the treeline marks its course, crossed Kiln Lane, into another field on a hedgeline and went through Otterbourne Park Wood where there is an agger laid with pebbles. South of the wood the Roman road crossed Allbrook Hill and the A335 to Eastleigh.

From Eastleigh the line of the Roman road is lost under development and the route probably continued southwards along or near Passfield Avenue at Fleming Park, then continued over a field where it is marked by a treeline to North Stoneham. At North Stoneham the route probably ran along the present road past the church and then the Roman road is lost under development from Swaythling to St Denys, going along the western side of the River Itchen on a ferry to the Roman town of Clausentum at Bitterne just east of the manor house.

7.1   ***The Winchester to Bitterne Roman road along the B3335 in Winchester.***

7.2 **The Roman road at St Cross where the main line railway tunnels through it.**

7.3 **Agger of the Roman road north of Compton.**

7.4   **The route along a minor road in South Down, Shawford.**

7.5   **The Roman road marked by a treeline in Otterbourne.**

7.6   ***The road as a treeline seen from Kiln Lane south of Otterbourne.***

7.7 *The Roman road along a treeline at North Stoneham.*

7.8 *Site of ferry across the Itchen on the Winchester to Bitterne Roman road at St Denys. The Roman town of Clausentum at Bitterne is behind the trees on the right.*

8. WINCHESTER TO WANBOROUGH
(43) 41½ miles

8.1 Agger of the Winchester to Wanborough Roman road alongside the B3420 in Winchester.

This Roman road which formed an important route to the Roman town of Corinium at Cirencester, left Winchester at the north gate and went in a north-westerley direction along the B3420 to Littleton and then along the A272 where it makes a slight change of direction at Worthy Down. At this point a milestone was found with an inscription on it. The main road follows it's course for about three miles to Hill Farm and then the B3420 marks its course again for ½ mile to Moody's Down Farm.

A footpath marks the route from the farm for two miles to Newton Stacey where it crossed the River Test and the B3048. It is marked by a footpath through the Harewood Forest, across a field on an agger on Cow Down and passes the Eastern end of the Andover road, where it crossed the Silchester to Old Sarum Roman road (Margary's No. 4b) at East Anton, the site of the Roman town of Leucomagus. North of this, the route is marked by footpaths and lanes through Hatherden, Tangley, and entered Wiltshire at Hampshire Gate.

From here the Roman road is known as Chute Causeway which is a magnificent agger in

8.2   The route along the B3420 at Harestock north of Winchester.

use as a modern road on a semi-circle to Tidcombe, where the north-westerly alignment resumes to the Roman town of Cunetio at Mildenhall via the Savernake Forest. North of Mildenhall, the route continued in a north-westerly direction to Wanborough where it joined the Speen to Cirencester Roman road. (Margary's No. 41b)

8.3   The straightness of the Roman road is evident along the present A272 at Hill Farm.

8.4 **The route along a footpath at Newton Stacey.**

8.5   *The Roman road at Newton Stacey where it crossed the River Test.*

8.6   *Agger of the Roman road across a field at Cow Down south of Andover.*

8.7   The Roman road at East Anton, Andover where it crossed the Portway on the site of the small Roman town of Leucomagus.

8.8   The Roman road along a footpath west of Enham Alamein.

8.9 The road along a footpath north of Hatherden.

8.10 The Winchester to Wanborough Roman road marked by a footpath and treeline at Downlands Farm near Tangley.

9. WINCHESTER TO OLD SARUM
(45a) 21½ miles

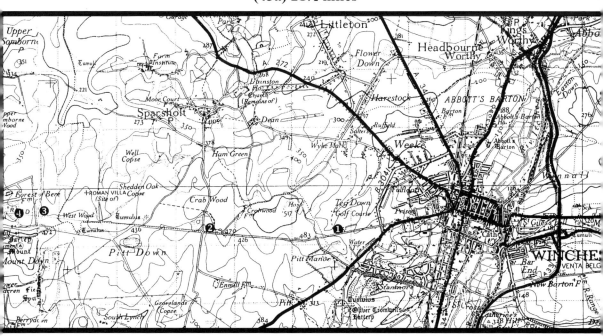

This route left Winchester at the West gate and went in a south-westerly direction along Sarum Road on Tegdown, and changed direction going north-westerly near Sarum Farm. West of this it ran just south of a minor road where it is visible as an agger at Crabwood Farm, then along the minor road north of Pitt Down. From here, the Roman road ran along the southern edge of West Wood on an agger and then it is marked as a chalk line and agger across fields at Forest of Bere Farm.

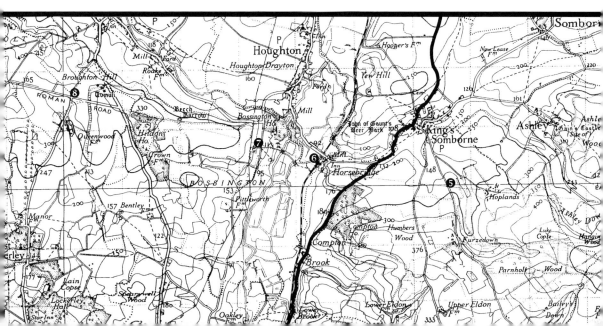

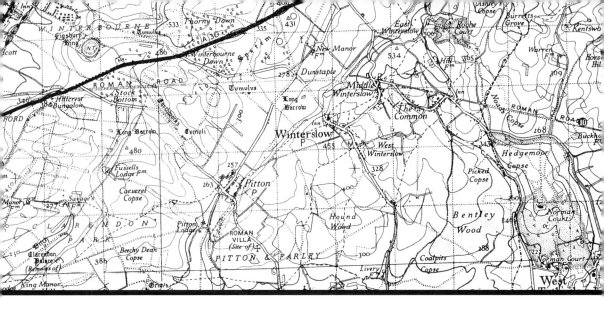

At the farm, the route ran along a minor road for about ¾ mile, then the Roman road climbed a deep combe on Ashley Down, then a footpath marks its course to Hoplands. At this point, the route crossed fields for about 1½ miles south of King's Somborne, crossed the A3057 where a footpath marks it for a short way, and crossed the old Test Valley railway just south of Horsebridge station where traces of a ridge and hedgerows mark its course.

West of Horsebridge the Roman road crossed the River Test on a ford by a footbridge and made a slight change of direction to the north-west passed Bossington, went across a field, and then a minor road marks it a mile or so south of Broughton for two miles. After

9.1 *The Winchester to Old Sarum Roman road along Sarum Road on Teg Down near Winchester.*

9.2   *The Roman road as a cutting at Crabwood Farm.*

this, the route is marked by a treeline, through a field to Buckholt Farm, and then along a minor road for a while, followed by a treelined agger to Little Buckholt Farm. West of this, the route is marked by a footpath along the northern end of Noad's Copse where it entered Wiltshire east of The Common.

The route went to the north of The Common along a footpath and a minor road to Middle Winterslow where it changed direction to the west, going along a footpath south of Firsdown and Stock Bottom. It continued along a lane from Bracknell Croft to Ford and entered the east gate of the Roman town of Sorviodunum at Old Sarum north of Salisbury.

9.3   *The road as a chalkline across a field east of Forest of Bere Farm.*

9.7   Agger of the route across a field at Bossington.

Left:

9.4   Agger of the Roman road across a field at Forest of Bere Farm.

9.5   Site of the road across a field south of King's Somborne.

9.6   Site of the Roman road marked as traces of a ridge and hedgerows at Horsebridge.

9.8   The Roman road along a minor road south of Broughton.

9.9   The route of the Roman road along a treeline east of Buckholt Farm.

9.10   The Winchester to Old Sarum Roman road along a treeline west of Buckholt Farm.

10. CHICHESTER TO SILCHESTER
(155) 39 miles

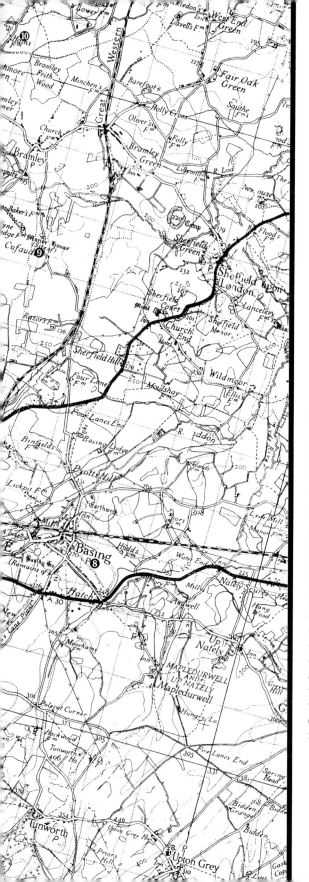

This Roman road left Chichester at the north gate went in a north-westerly direction through Lavant, over Heathbarn Down (where it is clearly visible on air photographs), and descended the South Downs at Linch Ball. The route then went across Iping Common, Iping Marsh where there is the site of a posting station (earthworks still visible in fields), through Milland Village and entered Hampshire north of Langley.

At Langley, the route changed direction near Weavers Down, passed through Longmoor, and changed direction again north-east of Greatham. The Roman road had a change of direction quite a few times on its southern course, but from Blackmoor, north of Greatham, it ran on a dead straight alignment in a north-westerly direction all the way to Silchester. North of Blackmoor, the road ran along a minor road at Chapel Farm, Oakhanger. After this it went across fields on aggers and through woodland near Shortheath, East Worldham, Wyck and through Neatham north-east of Alton.

At Neatham is the site of a small Roman town which is depicted by a hump in a field, and the Roman road is visible as an agger at this point. North of Neatham the route went through Cuckoo's Corner, over Holybourne Down on an agger, and then across fields at Swainshill Farm, Blounce, Dean Copse near South Wanborough, along a treeline south of Upton Grey and then through that village. North of this, the Roman road went to the west of Mapledurwell on a treeline and through fields, to the east of Basing, through Chineham and then a minor road marks its course through Cufaude. The route then went through Bramley, across fields, and joined the Silchester to Winchester Roman road (Margary's No. 42a) at Hains Farm about 1½ miles south of Silchester.

10.1   The Chichester to Silchester Roman road along a treeline at Blackmoor.

10.2   The Roman road visible as an agger across a field near East Worldham.

10.3   *The Roman road at the site of the small Roman town at Neatham near Alton.*

10.4   *The route as an agger across a field on Holybourne Down.*

10.5   Site of the Roman road across a field at Blounce.

10.6   The Roman road marked by a treeline north of Upton Grey.

10.7   **The Roman road on a hedgeline at Mapledurwell.**

10.8   **The route across a field at Old Basing.**

10.9   The road along a minor road through Cufaude

10.10   Site of the Chichester to Silchester Roman road at Hains Farm. It joined the Silchester to Winchester Roman road behind the farm buildings.

11. DORCHESTER TO SILCHESTER
(160c) 21 miles

This Roman road left the small Roman town at Dorchester (Oxfordshire) by the south gate and went in a south-easterly direction, crossing the River Thames near the present road bridge and then the Thames, where it went in a southerly direction along a hedgerow north of Brightwell. At Brightwell a sunken lane marks its course, it then went through Mackney, Chosley, and Moulsford where the A329 marks its course to Streatley (named from Roman road). It entered Berkshire about ½ mile north of Streatley Farm.

South of Streatley, the route probably ran along or near the A329 through the Thames Gap to Pangbourne, then changing direction to the south along the A340 through Tidmarsh, east of Englefield, west of Theale, and then crossed the River Kennet north of Sulhampstead. South of this, the route ran past Ufton Nervet, through woodland where it entered Hampshire, north west of Mortimer. The Roman road then crossed Chapel Road at Mortimer West End, ran along a track and treeline at West End Farm, went across a field and entered the Roman town of Calleva Atrebatum at Silchester at the north gate.

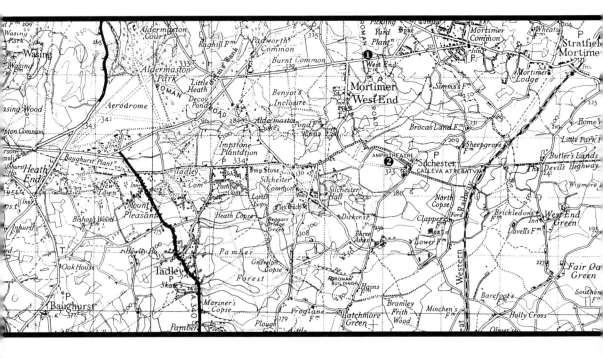

11.1   The Dorchester to Silchester Roman road as a treeline at West End Farm, Mortimer West End.

11.2   North gate of Calleva Atrebatum at Silchester where the Dorchester to Silchester Roman road entered the Roman town.

12. DORCHESTER TO FAIR CROSS
(160cc) 27 miles

This Roman road was probably an alternative route to Silchester via Henley-on-Thames. It left Dorchester at the south gate, went in a south-easterly direction through Benson where an airfield was built on its line, then a lane marks it at Harcourt Hill, went through Nettlebed and Henley-on-Thames where the Verulanium (St. Albans) to Henley Roman road (Margary's No. 163) joined it. The route of the latter is unknown west of the Thames crossing at Hedsor near Bourne End.

South of Henley-on-Thames, the route went in a south-westerly direction through Wargrave (where it enters Berkshire), on to Sonning and Reading through Whiteley and Spencers Woods. From here the Roman road is marked by a minor road for a short while, and then a footpath marks its course for about 1½ miles to Fair Cross where it entered Hampshire along a minor road for about ½ mile. At this point, the Roman road joined the London to Silchester route (Margary's No. 4a) at Home Farm, Fair Cross some 3½ miles east of Silchester.

It is possible that Roman road No. 163 could have been the Verulamium to Silchester Roman road making a direct link between the Roman towns, and the section of Roman road No. 160cc may have been the Dorchester to Henley-on-Thames Roman road, joining the former at Henley-on-Thames. Further research by future archaeologists may reveal this one day.

12.1   The Dorchester to Fair Cross Roman road along a minor road at Fair Cross.

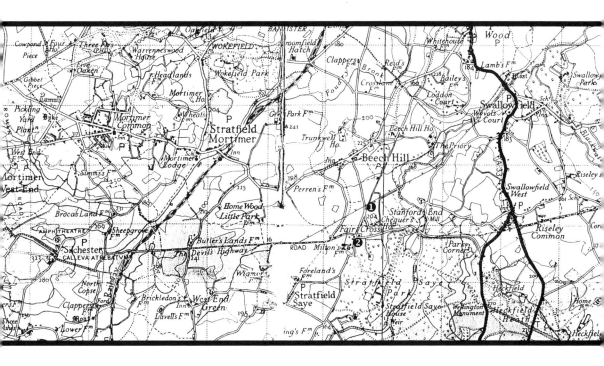

12.2   The Dorchester to Fair Cross Roman road along the minor road where it joined the London to Silchester road at Home Farm, Fair Cross.

13. WINCHESTER TO WICKHAM
(420) 12¼ miles

This Roman road left the Roman town of Venta Belgarum at Winchester at the east gate and went in a south-easterly direction along Chesil Street, Bar End Road and then over Twyford Down along Morestead Road where it turned more to the south-east at Deacon Hill. From here, the route is still marked by Morestead Road over Morestead Down, goes through Morestead village, then runs along a minor road in a cutting at Hill Farm to Owslebury.

At Owslebury, the Roman road ascended the hill on a terraceway, went across a field on a treeline, then a footpath marks its course where traces of agger are visible in places. South of this, the route went past Phillips Farm into Austin's Copse where it exists as an agger, after which it went across fields east of Rowhay Farm to Upham Farm. From here the route is marked by another footpath, then a minor road for a short way. After crossing the B2177 another footpath marks its course to Wintershill.

South of Wintershill, the Roman road is visible as a terraceway across a field west of Bishop's Waltham, it went through Tangier and Brooklands Farms, and crossed the B3035 road where it appears as a hollow way in a field north of Harfields Farm. From here the route went across fields west of Waltham Chase, ran along or near Sandy Lane, through Shedfield where it is marked by a footpath, then across a field north-west of Wickham and joined the Chichester to Bitterne Roman road (Margary's No. 421) in Wickham. This route and route 421 from Wickham provided a direct route from Winchester to Chichester.

13.1 The Winchester to Wickham Roman road along a lane and footpath in Winchester.

13.2 The Roman road where it changed direction along Morestead Road at Deacon Hill.

13.3 The route along Morestead Road at Morestead Farm.

13.4   Terraceway of the Roman road as it ascends a hill at Owslebury.

13.5   The route marked by a treeline across fields south of Owslebury.

13.6 *Agger of the Roman road at Austin's Copse south of Phillips Farm.*

13.7 *Terraceway of the Roman road across a field south of Wintershill.*

13.8   *Hollow way of the road north of Harfields Farm near Bishop's Waltham.*

13.9   *Agger of the Roman road in woodland north of Shedfield.*

13.10   *The Winchester to Wickham Roman road as a mark across a field in Wickham.*

14. CHICHESTER TO BITTERNE
(421) 27½ miles

This Roman road left Chichester at the west gate and went either westwards through Fishbourne to Bosham or north-west to Ratham Mill, then south-west along Mudberry Lane to Bosham. The route west of Bosham is self evident going along the A259 through Nutbourne, Southbourne and entering Hampshire at Emsworth, where it ran along the main and then a minor road through Havant where it is marked by a bend opposite the Bear Hotel in East Street.

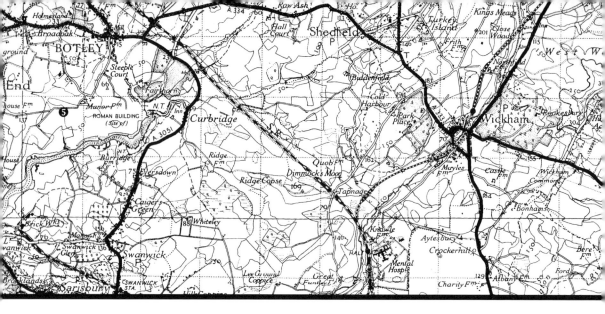

The route then crossed North and South Streets (a possible Roman road in a small Roman town) by Havant church, ran along West Street which is now a shopping precinct, and changed direction to the north-west, along roads through Bedhampton. From here the route is lost under development to Purbrook, then went across a field and along a minor road, through woodland to Southwick where there is a treelined agger.

The B2177 marks its course north-west of Southwick at Waltham Heath to North Boarhunt, then few traces of the route are visible from here to Botley. It may have run on a straight course south of the B2177 through Wickham Common (where there is an agger), and probably changed direction

14.1   The Chichester to Bitterne Roman road along the A259 in Emsworth.

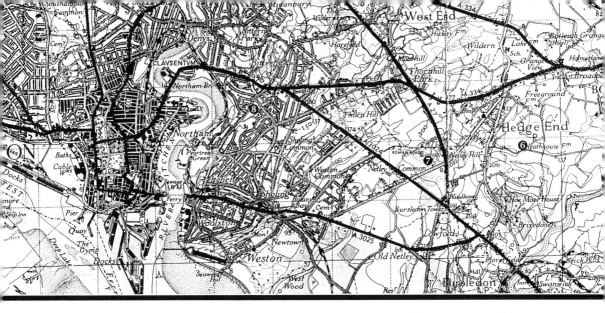

to the west after crossing the River Meon where the Winchester to Wickham Roman road (Margary's No. 420) joined it at Wickham. From here the route went through fields and woodland, crossed the River Hamble at Curbridge near Botley, and ran along a footpath and treeline to Hedge End.

The Roman road is lost under development through Hedge End, ran across a field and the M27 crosses its line on Netley Hill. The route crossed Netley Common by a tumulus, went through a built up area through Sholing Common, and then traces of an agger are visible on Freemantle Common in Bitterne, where a plaque marks its site. The Roman road then runs over Lances Hill to the Roman town of Clausentum which is now occupied by the Bitterne Manor area.

14.2   The Roman road along East and West Streets in Havant at the site of the small Roman town.

14.3   *The road marked by a treeline at Purbrook.*

14.4   *Agger of the Roman road in a field at Southwick.*

14.5   ***The route marked by a footpath south of Botley.***

14.6   *The Roman road marked by a treeline across a field near Hedge End.*

14.7   *Line of the Roman road on Netley Common immediately behind the Tumulus on the right.*

14.8   Plaque marking the site of the Chichester to Bitterne Roman road on Freemantle Common in Bitterne.

15. OTTERBOURNE TO STONEY CROSS
(422) 15 miles

This Roman road branched off the Winchester to Bitterne Roman road (Margary's No. 42b) in Otterbourne near the Forge Inn and went in a south-westerly direction along a minor road through Otterbourne to Otterbourne Hill, where the M3 crosses its line. After this, the route ran along Winchester Road in Chandler's Ford for about a mile and then its course is lost under development.

South of Chandler's Ford, the Roman road is visible as an agger and cutting across a field at Velmore Farm. It then passed through Hut Wood, ran through Chilworth where it crossed the A27 near the Clump Inn, and then the M27 crosses its line south of the village. South of the M27, the line of the Roman road is marked by a footpath for a while and then it went through a built up area at Rownhams and Nursling, where there was a Roman settlement. At Nursling the Roman road crossed the River Test.

After the river crossing, the route crossed the A36, went through woodland south of Stoneyford, Barrow Hill and is visible as an agger across a field at Copythorne. It passed some 200 yards south of Copythorne Church to Cadnam and then ran along the A31 to Stoney Cross where the Stoney Cross to Fritham Roman road (Margary's No. 424) probably joined it.

It is possible that this Roman road continued further westwards to Wimborne via Ringwood either along the A31 or on a straight alignment near it. There is a short length of agger at Park Farm a mile east of Wimborne. Wimborne Road through Ferndown, which is very straight, may also mark a Roman road. It probably joined the Badbury Rings to Poole Harbour Road (Margary's No. 4d) at Lambs Green near Wimborne.

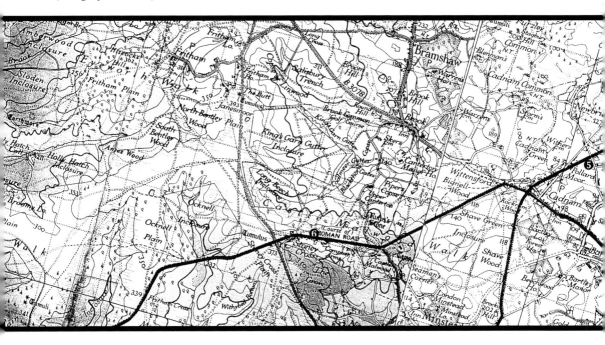

15.1   Otterbourne to Stoney Cross Roman road in Otterbourne where it joined the Winchester to Bitterne Roman road behind The Old Forge Inn.

15.2   The Roman road along a minor road through Otterbourne.

15.3   Cutting of the Roman road across fields at Velmore Farm near Chilworth.

15.4   The Roman road marked by a treeline at Stoneyford.

15.5   Agger of the Roman road across a field at Copythorne.

15.6   Line of the Otterbourne to Stoney Cross Roman road along the A31 at Stoney Cross.

16. DIBDEN TO LEPE
(423) 7 miles

This Roman road ran along the western shore of the Southampton Water and it is marked by a minor road called "Roman Road" at Dibden which runs parallel with the A326 to Dibden Purlieu. At Dibden Purlieu the Roman road changed direction to the south-east where it is visible as a well preserved agger (21 feet wide and two feet high) on Fawley Inclosure from near Hardley to Little Holbury. From the latter place, the route crossed a field, then marked by a footpath west of Blackfield, and then it is visible as an agger on Blackfield Common.

South of Blackfield, the route ran along the present road for about a mile from Langley, past Whitefield Farm, went across a field and then it is marked by a farm road from Stone Farm to Stone Point at Lepe. At Stone Point it is likely that a ferry existed to the Isle of Wight to a point near Cowes, where Rew Street (suggestive name) may be on or near the line of a possible Roman road, linking the Roman villas and other settlements on the Isle of Wight with those on the main land.

It is also possible that the Dibden to Lepe Roman road continued further northwards from Dibden to Totton via Marchwood to join the Otterbourne to Stoney Cross Roman road (Margary's No. 422). It could also have turned to the north-east at Dibden to cross the River Test, possibly on a ferry, to Southampton and then forded the River Itchen near Northam Bridge to the Roman town of Clausentum at Bitterne.

16.1   *The Dibden to Lepe Roman road in Dibden Purlieu.*

16.2   Outstanding agger of the Roman road on Fawley Inclosure.

16.3   Agger of the Roman road on Blackfield Common.

16.4   *The Roman road along the present road at Whitefield Farm.*

16.5   *The Roman road along a farm road at Stone Farm.*

16.6   *Site of possible ferry on the Dibden to Lepe Roman road across the Solent to the Isle of Wight at Stone Point, Lepe.*

17. STONEY CROSS TO FRITHAM
(424) 1½ miles

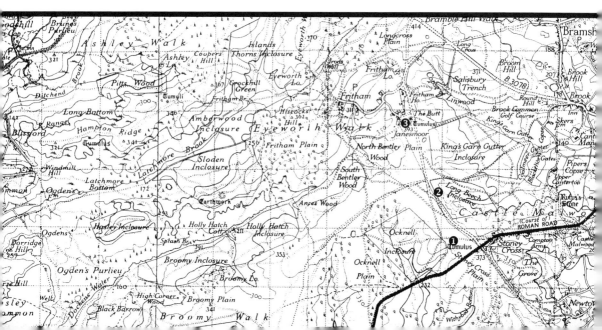

17.1   Site of the Stoney Cross to Fritham Roman road in heather at Stoney Cross.

This short length of Roman road probably branched off the Otterbourne to Stoney Cross Roman road (Margary's No. 422) at Little Stoney Cross. The route went northwards to Fritham, west, then east, then west again of a minor road. The first section of the road is clearly seen in heather where there is a low agger, but the rest of the route has been lost under an aerodrome which is no more, west of Long Beech Inclosure.

17.2   Site of the Roman road at Long Beech Inclosure.

It is possible that this Roman road went further north to Old Sarum via Redlynch and Alderbury, but no traces of an aligned road have been discovered. It is also possible that it went south-eastward to Dibden via Emery Down to connect with Roman road Margary's No. 423 to Lepe. This would make the junction at Little Stoney Cross a Roman crossway with a possible Roman settlement.

17.3   Site of the Stoney Cross to Fritham Roman road at Fritham.

18.   OTHER ROMAN ROADS AND TRACKS

There are probably many more Roman roads still to be discovered in Hampshire. One possible Roman road is from Winchester, leaving the Roman town of Venta Belgarum at the east gate, going eastwards along the B3404, passing Magdalen Down, Morn Hill, and then along the A31 at Chilcomb Down. From here it probably went to the north-east to the small Roman town at Neatham near Alton via Old Alresford and Medstead. It either joined the Chichester to Silchester Roman road (Margary's No. 155), or it crossed it at Neatham and went further north-eastwards towards London via Farnham and Woking, making a more direct London to Winchester Roman road.

Alternatively this route may have changed direction to the south-east to join Roman road No. 155 at the Iping posting station, via Bramdean and Stoner Hill near High Cross, where there is the site of a Romano-British settlement near Wheeler's Farm. This Roman road may also have gone to the Hardham posting station on Stane Street via Midhurst and Petworth. It is also possible that this Roman road provided an important east-west route from Pevensey (Anderida) to Charterhouse in the Mendips via Roman road Nos. 140, 142, 145, 45a and 45b.

Another Roman road is from Hayling Island to the South Downs via Havant and Chalton. This would have served the Roman temple on Hayling Island and crossed Langstone Harbour

18.1   The conjectural Roman road from Winchester to Hardham along the B3404 at Morn Hill east of Winchester.

18.2   The line of the Roman road along the A31 near Chilcomb Down.

18.3   ***The Hayling Island to Chalton Roman road at Langstone where it crossed the harbour on either a ferry or causeway known as "The Wadeway."***

18.4   ***The Roman road along a treeline at Langstone.***

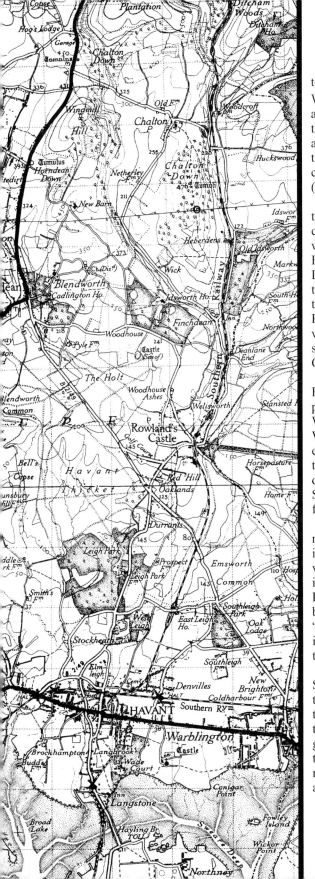

to Langstone village either on a ferry or the Wadeway which was a track about ¾ mile long and may have been used as a causeway. From the village the route went northwards across a field where a treeline possibly marks it and then along South and North Street in Havant, crossing the Chichester to Bitterne Roman road (Margary's No. 421) by the parish church.

At Havant there was a small Roman town with a Market in the vicinity of the crossways and Roman foundations and tiles were found beneath the church. North of Havant, the Roman road went through West Leigh, Rowlands Castle, Finchdean, and onto the South Downs at Chalton where there is the site of a sizeable Roman settlement. This Roman road either joined other trackways or went further north, perhaps to the Iping posting station via Petersfield where a road called "The Causeway" may be on its line.

A Roman road may have gone to the Roman fort at Portchester (Portus Adurni), probably an extension of the Winchester to Wickham route (Margary's No. 420) from Wickham. It would have gone in a south-easterly direction via Crockerhill, crossed the Wallington River at Whitedell Farm, over downland near Boarhunt, possibly along Castle Street in Portchester and then entered the Roman fort at the north west gate.

The number of trackways are too numerous to mention here, but one of them is the North Downs Ridgeway, which was a very ancient trackway and was probably used in Neolithic times or even earlier. It goes from Dover in Kent through to Wiltshire. It was used by the Romans and parts of it are known as "The Pilgrims Way" which is a name given to it in medieval times for the Pilgrims who travelled to Canterbury and Winchester along it.

Another ancient trackway is the South Downs Way, which was also used by the Neolithic people and possibly earlier. This trackway went from Eastbourne in East Sussex to Winchester and probably beyond. The high ground was preferred by early civilizations and the Romans also used this route. Several Roman roads crossed both the North Downs Ridgeway and the South Downs Way.

18.5   The Roman road along South and North Streets in Havant where it crossed the Chichester to Bitterne Roman road in the small Roman town.

18.6   Possible route of the Roman road along a footpath over the South Downs at Chalton Down.

18.7   The South Downs Way on Butser Hill.

18.8   The South Downs Way near Temple Valley east of Winchester.

MP **Middleton Press**

Easebourne Lane, Midhurst, West Sussex.
GU29 9AZ Tel:01730 813169

EVOLVING THE ULTIMATE RAIL ENCYCLOPEDIA

www.middletonpress.co.uk   email:info@middletonpress.co.uk
A-0 906520   B-1 873793   C-1 901706   D-1 904474

OOP Out of Print at time of printing - Please check current availability   **BROCHURE AVAILABLE SHOWING NEW TITLES**